SWITZERLAND
TRAVEL GUIDE 2024

A Pocket size guide for exploring the
Swiss top iconic landmarks, delightful
cuisine and off the beaten path of
Switzerland

GW00480595

JAMES D. FLICK

SWITZERLAND MAP

TABLE OF CONTENT

CHAPTER FIVE: EXPLORING SWISS LANDMARKS AND ATTRACTIONS _____ 37

CHAPTER SIX: OVERVIEW OF SWISS CUISINE _____ 77

CHAPTER SEVEN: EXPERIENCES AND ACTIVITIES IN SWITZERLAND 83

INTRODUCTION

Once upon a time, in a land embraced by the towering Alps and adorned with emerald valleys, there existed a place that seemed straight out of a fairy tale - Switzerland. Picture-perfect landscapes stretched as far as the eye could see, with rolling hills blanketed in lush greenery, crystal-clear lakes mirroring the azure skies, and snow-capped peaks kissing the heavens.

As the golden sun painted the horizon, it cast its enchanting glow upon quaint villages tucked between hillsides, each with charming chalets adorned with flower boxes bursting with vibrant blooms. The air was alive with the soothing melody of cowbells echoing from grazing pastures, while the aroma of freshly baked bread and rich Swiss chocolate wafted through the narrow streets.

But Switzerland was more than just postcard-perfect scenery; it was a land of captivating tales and timeless wonders. Majestic castles stood proudly, whispering stories of ancient knights and noble quests. Located within the verdant embrace of the forests were hidden trails leading to secret waterfalls and mystical grottos, inviting adventurers to uncover their mysteries.

In the heart of the cities, where modernity met tradition, the rhythm of life pulsed with precision and warmth. Cafés buzzed with laughter as locals savored their fondue and hearty raclette, sipping on velvety Swiss hot chocolate. Streets adorned with luxury boutiques and watchmakers' ateliers invited visitors to witness Swiss craftsmanship at its finest.

The allure of Switzerland was not just in its natural splendor; it was in the warmth of its people, the richness of its culture, and the harmony of tradition and innovation. Every corner of this magical land whispered tales of beauty, adventure, and a deep-rooted connection to nature.

And so, dear traveler, as you embark on your Swiss journey, prepare to be embraced by the charm of its landscapes, enthralled by its tales, and captivated by the timeless beauty that paints Switzerland as a living, breathing fairy tale waiting to be explored.

CHAPTER ONE: OVERVIEW OF SWITZERLAND

Switzerland, often described as a land of timeless beauty and precision, is a country that effortlessly weaves together natural splendor, cultural richness, and technological prowess. Located snugly in the heart of Europe, this small yet captivating nation has carved its mark on the world stage through a myriad of facets.

Landscapes

At the heart of Switzerland lies its most iconic feature—the majestic Swiss Alps. Towering peaks adorned with snow, alpine meadows adorned with wildflowers, and glacial lakes of astonishing clarity create a mesmerizing backdrop. The allure of these mountains extends far beyond their visual appeal; they offer a playground for adventure seekers, hosting world-class skiing in winter and unparalleled hiking in summer.

Venture beyond the Alps, and you'll encounter rolling hills, lush valleys, and serene lakes that seem almost surreal in their pristine beauty. Lake Geneva's elegance, Lake Lucerne's serenity, and the azure waters of Lake Constance beckon visitors to lose themselves in nature's embrace.

Culture and Heritage

Switzerland's cultural landscape is as diverse as its terrain. The country proudly preserves its heritage while embracing modernity. Each canton boasts its own traditions, languages, and customs, adding to the vibrant tapestry of Swiss culture.

From the charming Alpine villages where traditional festivals and folk music resonate with age-old traditions to the bustling cities where art, music, and innovation thrive, Switzerland seamlessly marries the old with the new.

Innovation and Precision

Renowned globally for its precision engineering, Switzerland sets the benchmark in craftsmanship and innovation. The Swiss watchmaking industry symbolizes this excellence, crafting timepieces that aren't just functional but also represent artistry and meticulous attention to detail.

Furthermore, Switzerland stands at the forefront of scientific research, boasting renowned universities and research institutes that foster innovation and technological advancements across various fields.

Swiss Culture and Heritage

Switzerland's cultural identity is a rich tapestry woven from various threads of history, tradition, and linguistic diversity. The country's unique position at the crossroads of several European cultures has shaped its distinct identity.

The Swiss hold dear their regional traditions and customs, evident in the vibrant festivals and folklore that dot the calendar. From the lively Fasnacht celebrations in Basel to the solemn Alp Abzug ceremonies in mountainous regions, these traditions are a testament to the Swiss reverence for their heritage.

Language and Multiculturalism

Switzerland's multilingual nature adds depth to its cultural fabric. The official languages of the nation are German, French, Italian, and Romansh. Each language corresponds to different regions, adding a dynamic linguistic landscape to the country.

This diversity extends beyond language, encompassing culinary traditions, music, arts, and literature, contributing to the country's rich tapestry of cultural expression.

Arts, Literature, and Innovation

Switzerland has fostered a fertile ground for artistic expression and innovation. From the classic literature of authors like Friedrich Dürrenmatt and Max Frisch to the avant-garde art showcased in museums and galleries, the

Geography and Climate

Switzerland's geographical diversity is nothing short of breathtaking. Located   within the heart of Europe, the country's landscape comprises the majestic Alps dominating the southern and central regions and the rolling hills and plateaus extending to the north.

Numerous lakes, such as Lake Geneva, Lake Zurich, and Lake Constance, punctuate the terrain, offering stunning vistas and recreational opportunities. Rivers meander through valleys, carving out picturesque landscapes that attract visitors from around the world.

Varied Climate

The Swiss climate is as diverse as its landscape, with variations influenced by altitude and geographic location. The Alpine regions experience colder temperatures and heavier precipitation, ideal for winter sports enthusiasts. The lowlands and valleys enjoy a milder climate, experiencing warm summers and crisp winters.

Switzerland's climate showcases the vivid beauty of four distinct seasons, each painting a unique backdrop to the country's natural wonders, offering travelers an ever-changing canvas of scenic beauty throughout the year.

CHAPTER TWO: PLANNING YOUR SWISS ADVENTURE

Switzerland, with its diverse landscapes and array of activities, offers a unique experience throughout the year, planning for trip is crucial for a successful journey.

Best Time to Visit Switzerland

Switzerland, with its diverse landscapes and array of activities, offers a unique experience throughout the year. The best time to visit largely depends on your interests and what you wish to explore during your Swiss sojourn.

Spring (March to May): Blossoming Beauty

Spring in Switzerland brings a sense of renewal as nature awakens from its winter slumber. The months of March to May herald the blooming of vibrant flowers across the countryside, transforming the landscape into a colorful tapestry.

During spring, the weather gradually warms up, making it an ideal time for hiking, sightseeing, and exploring the picturesque towns without the peak tourist crowds. While the higher Alpine regions might still have some snow, lower altitudes experience pleasant temperatures.

Summer (June to August): Alpine Adventures

Summer is the pinnacle of outdoor adventures in Switzerland. The months of June to August offer long, sunlit days perfect for hiking, cycling, and exploring the stunning trails that crisscross the Swiss Alps. This season is also ideal for water sports on the numerous lakes, from paddleboarding to leisurely boat cruises.

Switzerland's cities and towns come alive with festivals, open-air concerts, and cultural events during the summer months, providing a glimpse into the vibrant Swiss culture.

Autumn (September to November): Golden Hues and Tranquility

Autumn casts a spell of tranquility and enchantment across Switzerland. As the trees don their golden hues, the landscape transforms into a picturesque canvas. September to November is an excellent time for hiking, as the trails are quieter, offering serene views of the changing foliage.

This season also marks the grape harvest in some regions, inviting visitors to indulge in wine tours and enjoy local culinary festivals celebrating the harvest.

Winter (December to February): Winter Wonderland

Switzerland's winter is synonymous with a fairytale-like ambiance. The snowy landscapes and world-class ski resorts beckon winter sports enthusiasts from across the globe. The months of December to February offer excellent skiing, snowboarding, and other winter activities in the Alps.

The Swiss Christmas markets, adorned with twinkling lights and festive cheer, add a magical touch to the winter experience, making it an ideal time for travelers seeking a cozy and enchanting holiday ambiance.

In essence, the best time to visit Switzerland depends on your preferences and the experiences you seek. Whether it's the blossoming spring, vibrant summer, serene autumn, or enchanting winter, Switzerland casts its spell in every season, promising an unforgettable adventure tailored to your desires.

Visas and Entry Requirements

While the allure of Switzerland is undeniable, understanding the visa and entry requirements is essential for a seamless travel experience. As a Schengen Area member, Switzerland implements a unified visa policy, simplifying the process for visitors from eligible countries.

Citizens of over 60 countries, including the United States, Canada, Australia, and most European Union nations, enjoy visa-free entry for stays of up to 90 days within a 180-day period. However, starting in May 2025, all visa-exempt visitors will need to register for an ETIAS (European Travel Information and Authorization System) prior to their trip. This online application is expected to be a quick and straightforward process, ensuring a hassle-free experience for most travelers.

For those not eligible for visa-free entry, the visa application process is relatively straightforward. The required documents typically include a valid passport, proof of financial means, travel insurance, and a completed visa application form. The processing time for visas varies depending on the applicant's nationality and circumstances.

As an avid traveler myself, I vividly recall the process of applying for a Swiss visa. While initially apprehensive, I found the procedure to be quite streamlined. The online application form was user-friendly, and the required documents were clear and concise. The visa was processed within the expected timeframe, allowing me to embark on my Swiss adventure without any delays.

Tips for a Smooth Entry into Switzerland

To ensure a smooth entry into Switzerland, consider these helpful tips:

- Ensure that your passport remainsis valid for at least threesix months beyond your planned departure date from the Schengen Area. Additionally, having.

- Have sufficient financial means to support yourself during your stay.

- Purchase travel insurance that includes medical coverage and repatriation.

- Complete the ETIAS application (if applicable) well in advance of your trip.

- Familiarize yourself with Swiss customs regulations and prohibited items.

With the visa and entry requirements in mind, you can now confidently plan your Swiss escapade. Whether you're planning to conquer the slopes of Zermatt, explore the charming streets of Bern, or indulge in the culinary delights of Zurich, Switzerland awaits with open arms. Embrace the adventure, immerse yourself in the culture, and create memories that will last a lifetime.

Budgeting Tips for Travelers

Accommodation

Switzerland offers a wide range of accommodations catering to various budgets. From luxury hotels to hostels and guesthouses, travelers can find options that suit their preferences. Budget-conscious travelers may consider staying in hostels, budget hotels, or exploring alternatives like Airbnb or vacation rentals for more affordable options.

Transportation

Switzerland boasts an efficient public transportation system, including trains, buses, and boats that connect cities, towns, and even remote mountain areas. Consider purchasing a Swiss Travel Pass or regional passes for unlimited travel within a specified period, offering great value for exploring the country.

Food and Dining

While dining out in Switzerland can be relatively expensive, travelers can save by opting for local markets, grocery stores, and bakeries for affordable meal options. Additionally, lunch menus at restaurants often offer better value than dinner menus.

Activities and Sightseeing

Many of Switzerland's natural attractions, such as hiking trails and scenic landscapes, are free to explore. Consider investing in city passes or museum passes to save on entrance fees to popular attractions and cultural sites.

Additional Tips

- Exchange currency at banks or use ATMs for better exchange rates than at airports or tourist spots.

- Take advantage of free walking tours or self-guided tours available in many cities.

- Consider traveling during the shoulder seasons (spring and autumn) to benefit from lower accommodation prices and fewer crowds.

CHAPTER THREE: GETTING TO AND AROUND SWITZERLAND

Transportation within Switzerland

Public Transportation

Switzerland boasts an exceptional public transportation network that's efficient, punctual, and well-connected. Trains, buses, trams, and boats operate seamlessly, covering cities, towns, and even the most remote alpine regions. Swiss Travel Passes, available for various durations, offer unlimited travel on the country's public transportation network, making it convenient for tourists to explore the country.

Trains

Switzerland's train system is renowned for its reliability and scenic routes. Swiss Federal Railways (SBB/CFF/FFS) operates most of the country's train services, connecting major cities and offering connections to neighboring countries like France, Germany, Italy, and Austria. The panoramic trains, such as the Glacier Express and Bernina Express, provide unforgettable journeys through breathtaking landscapes.

Buses and Trams

Buses complement the train network, reaching areas not covered by rail and providing connectivity within cities and towns. Major cities like Zurich, Geneva, and Bern have efficient tram systems, making it easy to navigate urban areas.

Boats and Ferries

Switzerland's lakeshores are adorned with boat services, offering scenic cruises and transportation between lakeside towns. Lake Geneva, Lake Zurich, Lake Lucerne, and Lake Constance provide picturesque journeys by boat.

Airports and Railway Connections

Airports

Switzerland has many international airports that serve as the country's entry points:

- Zurich Airport (ZRH): Switzerland's largest airport, well-connected to major cities worldwide.

- Geneva Airport (GVA): Located near the French border, serving as a primary gateway to western Switzerland and the Alps.

- Basel-Mulhouse-Freiburg Airport (BSL/MLH/EAP): Located near Basel, close to the borders of France and Germany.

Railway Connections

Switzerland's railway system seamlessly connects major cities and extends its reach to neighboring countries:

- Zurich Hauptbahnhof (Zurich HB): One of Europe's busiest train stations, serving as a crucial hub for national and international connections.

- Geneva Cornavin: Offering connections to France and major Swiss cities.

- Basel SBB: Strategically located near the borders of France and Germany, facilitating international travel.

The Swiss Travel System offers integrated tickets, allowing seamless transitions between trains, buses, boats, and even some mountain railways.

Public Transport in Switzerland

Trains

Switzerland's railway system is renowned for its efficiency, punctuality, and scenic routes. The Swiss Federal Railways (SBB/CFF/FFS) operates an extensive network connecting cities, towns, and even remote areas. Trains offer comfortable and picturesque journeys, with panoramic routes like the Glacier Express providing unforgettable experiences through the Alps.

Buses and Trams

Buses complement the train network, reaching areas not covered by rail and providing urban and regional connectivity. Major cities like Zurich, Geneva, Basel, and Bern have efficient tram systems, making it convenient to navigate within urban areas. The Swiss Travel Pass often covers buses and trams, offering unlimited travel within certain regions or zones.

Boats and Ferries

Switzerland's lakeshores are served by boat services, offering scenic cruises and transportation between lakeside towns. Lakes such as Geneva, Zurich, Lucerne, and Constance provide picturesque journeys by boat.

Renting Cars/Bikes in Switzerland

Renting Cars

Renting a car in Switzerland provides flexibility, especially for exploring off-the-beaten-path areas. International and local car rental companies operate at airports and major cities, offering a range of vehicle options. While driving in Switzerland is relatively straightforward due to well-maintained roads, it's important to note that mountain roads might be narrow and require cautious driving, especially in winter.

Renting Bikes

Switzerland is bike-friendly, with many cities providing bike-sharing systems and rental shops offering bicycles for leisurely rides or more adventurous mountain biking. Cycling trails crisscross the country, providing scenic routes suitable for various skill levels. Some regions offer e-bike rentals, enabling riders to explore the Swiss landscape with ease.

Considerations

- **Swiss Travel Pass:** For tourists planning to extensively use public transportation, consider the Swiss Travel Pass, offering unlimited travel on trains, buses, and boats within a specified period.

- **Traffic Rules:** Familiarize yourself with Swiss traffic regulations, especially if planning to drive. Speed limits, parking regulations, and road signs may differ from those in other countries.

- **Cycling Safety:** Wear appropriate safety gear, especially when cycling in mountainous areas, and adhere to traffic regulations when biking in cities.

CHAPTER FOUR: ACCOMMODATIONS IN SWITZERLAND

Hotels and Resorts

Switzerland offers a wide array of hotels and resorts catering to various preferences and budgets. From luxurious five-star accommodations to cozy boutique hotels, visitors can find diverse options across the country.

The Dolder Grand- Zurich

Location: Located   in Zurich's hilltops, The Dolder Grand offers breathtaking views of the city, Lake Zurich, and the Alps.

Description: This luxurious hotel seamlessly blends historic charm with modern sophistication. Its opulent rooms, adorned with contemporary art and stylish furnishings, provide an exquisite stay. The hotel features an award-winning spa offering rejuvenating treatments, an indoor pool, and exquisite dining options. Guests can relish culinary delights at the Michelin-starred restaurant or unwind in the serene surroundings of the expansive park.

Price Range: Starting at around $700 per night for a double room.

The Chedi Andermatt- Andermatt

Location: Situated in the heart of the Swiss Alps in Andermatt, this 5-star hotel offers a perfect gateway to the mountainous landscapes.

Description: The Chedi Andermatt exudes elegance with its alpine design and luxurious amenities. Guests are greeted with warm hospitality, spacious rooms adorned with contemporary Alpine chic décor, and stunning mountain views. The hotel boasts an exceptional spa, multiple restaurants offering diverse cuisines, and a wine and cigar library. Outdoor enthusiasts can explore nearby skiing areas or relax in the hotel's serene environment.

Price Range: Starting at around $1,200 per night for a double room.

Badrutt's Palace Hotel- St. Moritz

Location: Overlooking the pristine Lake St. Moritz and the Swiss Alps, Badrutt's Palace Hotel is an emblem of luxury in St. Moritz.

Description: With a rich history dating back to 1896, Badrutt's Palace Hotel blends traditional elegance with contemporary amenities. The hotel boasts lavish rooms and suites, several restaurants serving gourmet cuisine, and an exclusive spa offering rejuvenating treatments. Guests can indulge in outdoor activities such as skiing, ice skating, or simply bask in the hotel's grandeur while enjoying panoramic views of the Engadin Mountains.

Price Range: Starting at around $900 per night for a double room.

Please keep in mind that all prices are estimates and subject to change. Booking in advance and checking the hotel's official website for current rates and promotions is recommended.

Guesthouses and Bed & Breakfasts

Guesthouses:

Switzerland offers numerous guesthouses known for their cozy and hospitable ambiance. These accommodations often reflect the warmth of Swiss hospitality, providing a more intimate experience for travelers seeking a homely atmosphere.

Gasthaus Hirschen- Eglisau

Location: Situated in the picturesque town of Eglisau along the Rhine River, offering a tranquil setting and easy access to Zurich.

Description: Gasthaus Hirschen is a historic guesthouse dating back to the 16th century. It boasts cozy rooms adorned with traditional Swiss décor, providing a rustic yet comfortable atmosphere. Guests can savor homemade Swiss cuisine at the onsite restaurant, which prides itself on using fresh local ingredients. The riverside location allows for scenic walks along the Rhine or exploring the charming town.

Price Range: Starting at approximately $150 per night for a double room with breakfast included.

B&B Chalet La Rose- Zermatt

Location: Located in the renowned ski resort of Zermatt, offering stunning views of the Matterhorn.

Description: B&B Chalet La Rose is a cozy alpine chalet with personalized hospitality. The rooms are designed in a classic Swiss style, providing a warm and welcoming ambiance. Guests can enjoy a hearty breakfast each morning before heading out to explore the breathtaking surroundings. The chalet is a short walk from the village center and close to ski lifts for convenient access to the slopes.

Price Range: Starting at approximately $200 per night for a double room with breakfast included.

Gasthaus Rössli- Meiringen

Location: Located   in the picturesque town of Meiringen in the Bernese Oberland, surrounded by stunning mountain scenery.

Description: Gasthaus Rössli is a traditional Swiss guesthouse offering comfortable rooms and a homely atmosphere. The guesthouse prides itself on its authentic Swiss cuisine, serving hearty meals showcasing regional specialties. Guests can explore nearby attractions such as the Reichenbach Falls or engage in outdoor activities like hiking and skiing in the nearby mountains.

Price Range: Starting at approximately $120 per night for a double room with breakfast included.

Please keep in mind that all prices are estimates and subject to change. It's advisable to check the establishment's official website or contact them directly for current rates and availability.

Camping and Outdoor Accommodations
Campgrounds:

Switzerland offers a plethora of well-maintained campgrounds, ideal for outdoor enthusiasts seeking a closer connection to nature. These campgrounds cater to tents, campervans, and sometimes offer wooden cabins or pods for more comfort.

Camping Jungfrau- Lauterbrunnen

Location: Situated in the heart of the Bernese Oberland, surrounded by majestic mountains and waterfalls.

Description: Camping Jungfrau offers various accommodation options, including tent sites, caravan pitches, and cozy wooden chalets. Located in a scenic valley, campers wake up to breathtaking views of the surrounding peaks. The site provides modern facilities, including washrooms, laundry, and a supermarket. Outdoor enthusiasts can partake in hiking, paragliding, or exploring nearby attractions like the Staubbach Falls and Jungfraujoch.

Price Range: Tent pitches starting at approximately $30 per night.

Camping Manor Farm- Interlaken

Location: Situated on the shores of Lake Thun, offering stunning views of the lake and the surrounding mountains.

Description: Camping Manor Farm provides a serene lakeside camping experience with a variety of accommodation options, including tent pitches, mobile homes, and wooden pods. The campsite offers modern amenities, including a restaurant, playground, and water sports facilities. Guests can enjoy swimming in the crystal-clear waters of Lake Thun, cycling along the lakeshore, or exploring nearby towns like Interlaken.

Price Range: Tent pitches starting at approximately $25 per night.

Camping Lazy Rancho- Zweisimmen

Location: Tucked away in the rolling hills of the Simmental Valley, offering a peaceful rural setting.

Description: Camping Lazy Rancho provides a tranquil camping experience amidst nature. The site offers tent pitches and rental accommodations like Swiss-style tipis or cozy wooden cabins. Surrounded by meadows and forests, guests can enjoy horseback riding, hiking trails, and relaxation in a rustic setting. The campsite also hosts barbecue evenings and outdoor activities for families.

Price Range: Tent pitches starting at approximately $20 per night.

Please keep in mind that all prices are estimates and subject to change. It's recommended to check the camping sites' official websites or contact them directly for current rates, availability, and any specific requirements.

CHAPTER FIVE: EXPLORING SWISS LANDMARKS AND ATTRACTIONS

Iconic Swiss Landmarks

Matterhorn:

Soaring 4,478 meters (14,692 feet) into the Swiss sky, the Matterhorn stands as an iconic symbol of Alpine grandeur, its pyramid-shaped peak instantly recognizable around the world. Straddling the border between Switzerland and Italy, this mighty mountain has captivated adventurers and artists alike, inspiring countless stories, paintings, and poems.

The Matterhorn's sheer beauty and formidable presence have long challenged mountaineers seeking to conquer its summit. For many years, it remained unconquered, its treacherous slopes claiming the lives of several daring climbers. It wasn't until 1865 that Edward Whymper, along with a team of seven, finally reached the Matterhorn's peak, an achievement that marked a turning point in the history of mountaineering.

Important Information to Keep in Mind When Visiting

Getting There:

The Matterhorn region is easily accessible by train from various Swiss cities, including Zurich, Geneva, and Bern. International airports in Zurich and Geneva provide connections to cities worldwide.

Accommodation:

A wide range of accommodation options is available in Zermatt and Breuil-Cervinia, from luxury hotels to cozy guesthouses and budget hostels.

Activities:

In addition to mountaineering, hiking, and skiing, the Matterhorn region offers a variety of activities, including glacier treks, scenic helicopter flights, and cultural attractions.

Additional Tips:

- Check the weather conditions before planning your trip, as they can change rapidly in the mountains.

- Dress appropriately for the conditions, and be sure to wear proper footwear.

- Leave no evidence of your visit to the natural environment.

Embrace the Majesty of the Matterhorn

A visit to the Matterhorn region is an unforgettable experience, offering a chance to witness the beauty of the Alps, engage in thrilling adventures, and immerse yourself in a rich cultural heritage. So, embark on a journey to this majestic mountain and discover the magic that awaits.

Jungfraujoch- Top of Europe

Perched atop the formidable peaks of the Bernese Oberland, Jungfraujoch, aptly named "Top of Europe," stands as the highest railway station in the continent. Ascend to this breathtaking altitude of 3,454 meters (11,333 feet) and discover a realm of unparalleled beauty, where snow-capped mountains, pristine glaciers, and breathtaking panoramas await.

The journey to Jungfraujoch is an adventure in itself. Step aboard the Jungfrau Railway, a marvel of engineering that has been transporting passengers to this lofty destination since 1893. As you wind your way up the mountainside, marvel at the ever-changing scenery, from verdant valleys to rugged peaks, culminating in the awe-inspiring sight of the Jungfraujoch station emerging from the mountainside.

Important Information to Keep in Mind When Visiting

Opening Hours:

Jungfraujoch is open year-round, but some attractions and activities may be subject to seasonal availability.

Admission Fees:

Admission fees vary depending on the time of year and the activities you wish to participate in.

Getting There:

Jungfraujoch is easily accessible by train from Interlaken Ost via Grindelwald or Lauterbrunnen.

Additional Tips:

- Dress warmly, as temperatures can drop even in summer.

- Wear sunscreen and sunglasses to protect yourself from the high-altitude sun.

- Allow plenty of time for your visit, as there is much to see and do.

A journey to Jungfraujoch is an unforgettable experience, offering a glimpse into the heart of the Swiss Alps. From the exhilarating train ride to the breathtaking panoramas and thrilling activities, Jungfraujoch is a destination that will leave you feeling amazed and inspired. So, embark on an adventure to the "Top of Europe" and discover the magic that awaits.

Château de Chillon

Located between the serene shores of Lake Geneva, Château de Chillon stands as a timeless sentinel, a testament to centuries of history and grandeur. Its imposing stone walls, gracefully adorned with turrets and arched windows, whisper tales of bygone eras, inviting travelers to embark on a captivating journey through time.

Important Information to Keep in Mind When Visiting

Opening Hours:

Tuesday to Sunday: 10:00 AM - 5:00 PM

Closed on Mondays

Admission Fees:

Adults: CHF 12 (approximately $12.50 USD)

Students (16-25 years): CHF 8 (approximately $8.40 USD)

Children (6-15 years): CHF 6 (approximately $6.30 USD)

Getting There:

By car: The castle is easily accessible by car from Montreux or Villeneuve. Parking is available near the castle.

By public transportation: The castle is served by the CFF train station "Veytaux-Chillon" and bus lines from Montreux, Vevey, and Villeneuve.

Additional Tips:

- Audio guides are available in several languages, including English, French, German, and Italian.

- Visitors with impairments are also welcome to tour the castle.

- A restaurant and a souvenir shop are located within the castle grounds.

Château de Chillon is more than just a historical monument; it's a portal to a bygone era, a place where history comes alive. As you explore its ancient halls and imagine the lives that once unfolded within its walls, you'll find yourself enchanted by the timeless allure of this magnificent fortress. So, step into the pages of history and embark on an unforgettable journey through time at Château de Chillon, a treasure trove of stories waiting to be discovered.

Swiss National Park:

Located between the heart of the Swiss Alps, the Swiss National Park stands as a pristine wilderness wonderland, a realm of towering peaks, verdant valleys, and crystal-clear lakes. Established in 1914 as one of the oldest national parks in Europe, this protected area encompasses over 170 square kilometers of breathtaking scenery, offering a sanctuary for a diverse array of flora and fauna.

As you step into the Swiss National Park, you'll be greeted by a breathtaking panorama of natural beauty. Snow-capped mountains pierce the azure sky, their reflections shimmering in the tranquil waters of serene lakes. Lush meadows, carpeted with wildflowers, stretch as far as the eye can see, while ancient forests provide a home for a rich tapestry of plant and animal life.

Important Information to Keep in Mind When Visiting

Opening Hours:

The park is open all year, however some portions may be inaccessible owing to snow during the winter months.

Admission Fees:

There is no entrance fee to the park.

Getting There:

The park is easily accessible by car or public transportation from nearby towns and cities.

Additional Tips:

- Be sure to pack proper clothing and footwear for the weather conditions.

- Respect the park's natural environment and leave no trace of your visit.

- Take your time and savor the beauty of the park.

The Swiss National Park is a treasure trove of natural wonders, a place where you can truly connect with the wild heart of Switzerland. As you explore its diverse landscapes, encounter its enchanting wildlife, and immerse yourself in its serene atmosphere, you'll discover a world of unparalleled beauty and tranquility. So, embark on an unforgettable adventure into the Swiss National Park, and let its awe-inspiring scenery and rich biodiversity captivate your senses and leave you feeling refreshed and inspired.

Museums and Art Galleries

Kunsthaus Zürich

Located between the vibrant cityscape of Zürich, Kunsthaus Zürich stands as a beacon of artistic expression, a treasure trove of masterpieces that span centuries and continents. Its imposing structure, adorned with classical architecture and modern elements, hints at the rich tapestry of artistic experiences that await within.

Important Information to Keep in Mind When Visiting

Opening Hours:

Tuesday to Sunday: 10:00 AM - 5:00 PM

Closed on Mondays

Admission Fees:

Adults: CHF 25 (approximately $26.50 USD)

Students (16-25 years): CHF 15 (approximately $16.00 USD)

Children (6-15 years): CHF 10 (approximately $10.50 USD)

Getting There:

By car: The Kunsthaus is located in the heart of Zürich, easily accessible by car from all directions. Parking garages are nearby.

By public transportation: The Kunsthaus is served by the tram lines 2, 3, 8, and 11, as well as the bus lines 31, 33, and 47.

Additional Tips:

- Audio guides are available in several languages, including English, French, German, and Italian.

- The Kunsthaus is accessible to visitors with disabilities.

- A restaurant and a bookstore are located within the museum grounds.

The Kunsthaus Zürich is more than just a museum; it's a sanctuary for art lovers, a place where creativity and imagination reign supreme. As you wander through its galleries, let your senses be captivated by the beauty and power of art, and allow yourself to be transported into worlds beyond your imagination. So, embark on an artistic odyssey, and discover the timeless masterpieces that await you at the Kunsthaus Zürich, a testament to the enduring legacy of human creativity.

Fondation Beyeler

Located between the tranquil greenery of Riehen, just outside Basel, Fondation Beyeler stands as a beacon of modern and contemporary art. Its sleek, modern architecture, seamlessly blending into the surrounding landscape, hints at the innovative and groundbreaking masterpieces that await within.

Important Information to Keep in Mind When Visiting

Opening Hours:

Tuesday to Sunday: 10:00 AM - 5:00 PM

Closed on Mondays

Admission Fees:

Adults: CHF 28 (approximately $30 USD)

Students (16-25 years): CHF 20 (approximately $21.50 USD)

Children (6-15 years): CHF 15 (approximately $16 USD)

Getting There:

By car: Fondation Beyeler is easily accessible by car from Basel. Parking is available at the museum.

By public transportation: The museum is served by the bus lines 31, 33, and 60.

Additional Tips:

- Audio guides are available in several languages, including English, French, German, and Italian.

- Visitors with impairments are also welcome to tour the castle.

- A restaurant and a bookstore are located within the museum grounds.

Foundation Beyeler is an invitation to embark on a journey of artistic exploration, where the boundaries of creativity are constantly redefined. As you wander through its galleries, let your imagination soar, and allow yourself to be captivated by the power and beauty of art. From the timeless masterpieces of modern masters to the groundbreaking creations of contemporary artists, Fondation Beyeler offers an unparalleled immersion into the world of art, a testament to the enduring legacy of human creativity.

Swiss Museum of Transport

Located on the shores of Lake Lucerne, amidst the picturesque Swiss Alps, the Swiss Museum of Transport is a treasure trove of innovation and history, a testament to human ingenuity and our enduring fascination with mobility. As you step through its grand entrance, you'll be transported on an exhilarating journey through time and technology, traversing centuries of groundbreaking inventions and marveling at the wonders of transportation.

Important Information to Keep in Mind When Visiting

Opening Hours:

Daily: 9:00 AM - 5:00 PM

Admission Fees:

Adults: CHF 30 (approximately $32.50 USD)

Students (16-25 years): CHF 24 (approximately $26 USD)

Children (6-15 years): CHF 18 (approximately $19.50 USD)

Family ticket (2 adults and 2 children): CHF 84 (approximately $90 USD)

Getting There:

By car: The museum is easily accessible by car from Lucerne. Parking is available at the museum.

By public transportation: The museum is served by the Lucerne S-Bahn train line S5, with a stop at the adjacent Verkehrshaus railway station.

Additional Tips:

- Audio guides are available in several languages, including English, French, German, and Italian.
- Visitors with impairments are also welcome to tour the castle.
- Several restaurants and cafes are located within the museum grounds.

The Swiss Museum of Transport is more than just a museum; it's a journey of discovery and inspiration. As you explore its vast collection of exhibits, you'll gain a profound appreciation for the ingenuity and perseverance that have shaped the world of transportation. From the humble beginnings of human mobility to the cutting-edge technologies that are shaping our future, the Swiss Museum of Transport is a testament to the boundless human spirit and our continuing interest with the world around us.

Olympic Museum, Lausanne

Located   on the shores of Lake Geneva, amidst the picturesque Swiss Alps, the Olympic Museum stands as a beacon of sporting excellence, a testament to the enduring power of the Olympic spirit. As you step through its grand entrance, you'll be transported into a world of athletic prowess, where the stories of legendary athletes and iconic moments unfold before your eyes.

Important Information to Keep in Mind When Visiting

Opening Hours:

Tuesday to Sunday: 10:00 AM - 6:00 PM

Closed on Mondays

Admission Fees:

Adults: CHF 20 (approximately $22 USD)

Students (16-25 years): CHF 15 (approximately $16.50 USD)

Children (6-15 years): CHF 10 (approximately $11 USD)

Getting There:

By car: The museum is easily accessible by car from Lausanne. Parking is available at the museum.

By public transportation: The museum is served by the Lausanne metro line M2, with a stop at the Lausanne-Ouchy Olympique station.

Additional Tips:

- Audio guides are available in several languages, including English, French, German, and Italian.

- Visitors with impairments are also welcome to tour the castle.

- A restaurant and a gift shop are located within the museum grounds.

Embrace the Olympic Spirit

The Olympic Museum is an invitation to embrace the Olympic spirit, to celebrate the power of sport to inspire, unite, and transform lives. As you explore its captivating exhibits and immerse yourself in the stories of Olympic legends, you'll leave feeling empowered and inspired, ready to embrace your own personal journey of excellence and achievement.

Natural Wonders: Mountains, Lakes, and Parks

Eiger, Mönch, and Jungfrau

These three majestic peaks in the Bernese Alps near the town of Interlaken form an impressive trio. The Jungfrau Region offers stunning landscapes, hiking trails, and breathtaking views accessible via cogwheel trains, cable cars, and hiking routes.

The Eiger

The Eiger is the most famous of the three peaks, known for its sheer north face, which has claimed the lives of many climbers. The mountain's north face is one of the most challenging climbing routes in the world, and it has been the subject of numerous films and books.

The Mönch

The Mönch is the second-highest of the three peaks, and it is known for its elegant, pyramid-shaped summit. The mountain's name means "monk" in German, and it is said to resemble a monk's cowl.

The Jungfrau

The Jungfrau is the highest of the three peaks, and it is known for its panoramic views of the surrounding Alps. The mountain's name means "virgin" in German, and it is said to resemble a young woman's profile.

A Challenge for Mountaineers

The Eiger, Mönch, and Jungfrau are all popular destinations for mountaineers. The Eiger's north face is a particularly challenging climb, and it is only recommended for experienced climbers. The Mönch and Jungfrau are also challenging climbs, but they are less dangerous than the Eiger's north face.

Important Information to Keep in Mind When Visiting

Getting There:

The Eiger, Mönch, and Jungfrau region is easily accessible by train from various Swiss cities, including Zurich, Geneva, and Bern. International airports in Zurich and Geneva provide connections to cities worldwide.

Accommodation:

A wide range of accommodation options is available in Grindelwald, Lauterbrunnen, and Wengen, from luxury hotels to cozy guesthouses and budget hostels.

Activities:

In addition to mountaineering, hiking, and skiing, the Eiger, Mönch, and Jungfrau region offers a variety of activities, including glacier treks, scenic helicopter flights, and cultural attractions.

Additional Tips:

- Check the weather conditions before planning your trip, as they can change rapidly in the mountains.

- Dress appropriately for the conditions, and be sure to wear proper footwear.

- Respect the natural environment and leave no trace of your visit.

A visit to the Eiger, Mönch, and Jungfrau region is an unforgettable experience, offering a chance to witness the beauty of the Alps, engage in thrilling adventures, and immerse yourself in a rich cultural heritage. So, embark on a journey to these majestic peaks and discover the magic that awaits.

Matterhorn

As mentioned earlier, the Matterhorn in the Pennine Alps is an iconic and photogenic mountain, attracting climbers and visitors alike to its awe-inspiring beauty.

Lakes

Lake Geneva

Located between the picturesque landscapes of Switzerland and France, Lake Geneva, also known as Lac Léman, stands as a shimmering jewel set against the backdrop of the majestic Alps. Its crescent-shaped expanse stretches for 73 kilometers (45 miles), making it the largest lake in Western Europe and a natural playground for outdoor enthusiasts, art lovers, and those seeking a tranquil escape amidst breathtaking scenery.

Important Information to Keep in Mind When Visiting

Getting There:

Lake Geneva is easily accessible by train from major Swiss cities like Zurich and Bern, as well as from neighboring France. The Geneva International Airport provides connections to cities worldwide.

Accommodation:

A wide range of accommodation options is available around Lake Geneva, from luxurious hotels and spas to cozy bed and breakfasts and budget-friendly hostels.

Activities:

In addition to watersports, hiking, and biking, Lake Geneva offers a variety of activities, including wine tasting, vineyard tours, and cultural attractions.

Additional Tips:

- Learn a few basic French phrases, as many people around the lake speak both French and German.

- Check the weather conditions before planning your trip, as they can change rapidly in the mountains.

- Dress appropriately for the conditions, and be sure to wear comfortable shoes for walking and hiking.

Embrace the Serenity and Beauty of Lake Geneva

A visit to Lake Geneva is an invitation to immerse yourself in the natural beauty, cultural richness, and vibrant spirit of this region. Whether you're seeking invigorating outdoor adventures, captivating cultural experiences, or simply a tranquil escape, Lake Geneva offers a symphony of experiences that will leave you feeling refreshed, inspired, and deeply connected to the essence of this enchanting destination.

Lake Lucerne

Located between the majestic peaks of the Swiss Alps, Lake Lucerne, also known as Vierwaldstättersee in German, is a shimmering gem that has captivated travelers for centuries. Its pristine waters, verdant shorelines, and picturesque backdrop form a captivating setting for outdoor adventures, cultural explorations, and serene moments of reflection. As you embark on a journey through this enchanting region, prepare to be swept away by the lake's tranquil beauty, rich history, and abundance of natural wonders.

Important Information to Keep in Mind When Visiting

Getting There:

Lake Lucerne is easily accessible by train from major Swiss cities like Zurich and Bern. The Lucerne Airport provides connections to cities worldwide.

Accommodation:

A wide range of accommodation options is available around Lake Lucerne, from luxurious hotels and spas to cozy bed and breakfasts and budget-friendly hostels.

Activities:

In addition to watersports, hiking, and biking, Lake Lucerne offers a variety of activities, including boat tours, scenic train rides, and cultural attractions.

Additional Tips:

- Learn a few basic German phrases, as German is the primary language spoken in the region.

- Check the weather conditions before planning your trip, as they can change rapidly in the mountains.

- Dress appropriately for the conditions, and be sure to wear comfortable shoes for walking and hiking.

A journey to Lake Lucerne is an invitation to immerse yourself in the region's natural beauty, cultural richness, and tranquil atmosphere. Whether you're seeking invigorating outdoor adventures, captivating cultural experiences, or simply a peaceful escape amidst the Alps, Lake Lucerne offers a symphony of experiences that will leave you feeling refreshed, inspired, and deeply connected to the essence of this enchanting destination.

Swiss National Park

As mentioned earlier, the Swiss National Park in the Engadin Valley is Switzerland's oldest national park, offering pristine wilderness, hiking trails, and diverse flora and fauna amidst the stunning alpine landscape.

Nature Reserves and Regional Parks

Switzerland boasts several regional parks and nature reserves, such as the Entlebuch Biosphere Reserve and the Aletsch Arena, known for their biodiversity and natural beauty.

Hidden Gems and Off-the-Beaten-Path Places

Lauterbrunnen Valley

Located between the heart of the Swiss Alps, the Lauterbrunnen Valley is a breathtaking gorge showcasing cascading waterfalls, lush meadows, and towering peaks. Renowned for its natural beauty and diverse array of activities, the valley has long captivated adventurers, nature lovers, and those seeking a serene escape amidst stunning scenery.

Important Information to Keep in Mind When Visiting

Getting There:

The Lauterbrunnen Valley is easily accessible by train from Interlaken Ost, a major transportation hub in the Swiss Alps.

Accommodation:

A wide range of accommodation options is available in the valley, from luxurious hotels and spas to cozy bed and breakfasts and budget-friendly hostels.

Activities:

In addition to hiking, biking, and paragliding, the Lauterbrunnen Valley offers a variety of activities, including rock climbing, canyoning, and scenic train rides.

Additional Tips:

- Learn a few basic German phrases, as German is the primary language spoken in the region.

- Check the weather conditions before planning your trip, as they can change rapidly in the mountains.

- Dress appropriately for the conditions, and be sure to wear comfortable shoes for walking and hiking.

A journey to the Lauterbrunnen Valley is an invitation to immerse yourself in the region's natural beauty, cultural richness, and tranquil atmosphere. Whether you're seeking invigorating outdoor adventures, captivating cultural experiences, or simply a peaceful escape amidst the Alps, the Lauterbrunnen Valley offers a symphony of experiences that will leave you feeling refreshed, inspired, and deeply connected to the essence of this enchanting destination.

Appenzell

Appenzell, located in northeastern Switzerland, is a charming alpine canton known for its stunning scenery, rich culture, and vibrant traditions. The canton is divided into two half-cantons, Appenzell Innerrhoden and Appenzell

Ausserrhoden, each with its own unique character and charm.

A Land of Natural Beauty

Appenzell is a land of natural beauty, with a landscape that is dominated by the Alpstein mountain range. The mountains provide breathtaking vistas as well as hiking, biking, and other outdoor sports. The canton is also home to a number of lakes, including Lake Walen and Lake Constance.

Popular Tourist Destinations

Appenzell is a popular tourist destination, attracting visitors from all over the world. Some of the most popular tourist destinations in Appenzell include:

- Appenzell Town: The capital of Appenzell Innerrhoden, Appenzell Town is a charming medieval town with narrow streets, colorful houses, and a number of historical landmarks, including the Landhaus, the seat of the cantonal government.

- Hoher Kasten: A mountain overlooking the town of Appenzell, the Hoher Kasten offers stunning views of the surrounding area.

- Alpstein: A mountain range that straddles the border between Appenzell and St. Gallen, the Alpstein is a popular destination for hiking, biking, and other outdoor activities.

- Lake Walen: A lake located in the southeastern part of Appenzell, Lake Walen is a popular destination for swimming, boating, and fishing.

- Lake Constance: A large lake that straddles the border between Switzerland, Austria, and Germany, Lake Constance is a popular destination for swimming, boating, and other water activities.

Important Information to Keep in Mind When Visiting

Getting There:

Appenzell is easily accessible by train from major Swiss cities, including Zurich, Basel, and Bern. The Appenzell Railway provides connections to the canton's two half-cantons.

Accommodation:

A wide range of accommodation options is available in Appenzell, from luxurious hotels to cozy bed and breakfasts and budget-friendly hostels.

Activities:

In addition to hiking, biking, and swimming, Appenzell offers a variety of activities, including cheesemaking demonstrations, traditional festivals, and cultural tours.

Additional Tips:

- Learn a few basic German phrases, as German is the primary language spoken in the canton.

- Check the weather conditions before planning your trip, as the weather in the Alps can change rapidly.

- Dress appropriately for the conditions, and be sure to wear comfortable shoes for walking and hiking.

Embrace the Charm and Beauty of Appenzell

A visit to Appenzell is an invitation to immerse yourself in the canton's stunning scenery, rich culture, and vibrant traditions. Whether you're seeking a relaxing getaway in the Alps, a cultural adventure, or simply a chance to experience a unique corner of Switzerland, Appenzell has something to offer everyone.

Val Verzasca

Located   in the heart of the Swiss Alps, Val Verzasca is a hidden gem that is known for its stunning scenery, crystal-clear waters, and charming villages. The valley is a popular destination for outdoor enthusiasts, offering a variety of hiking, biking, and swimming opportunities.

Val Verzasca is a land of natural beauty, with a landscape that is dominated by the Verzasca River. The river flows through the valley, creating a series of waterfalls, gorges, and pools. The valley is also home to a number of alpine lakes, including Lake Maggiore.

Important Information to Keep in Mind When Visiting

Getting There:

Val Verzasca is easily accessible by car or train. The nearest train station is at Locarno, which is located at the southern end of the valley. From Locarno, you can take a bus or taxi to Lavertezzo, the main village in the valley.

Accommodation:

A wide range of accommodation options is available in Val Verzasca, from luxury hotels to cozy bed and breakfasts and budget-friendly hostels.

Activities:

In addition to hiking, biking, and swimming, Val Verzasca offers a variety of activities, including canyoning, rock climbing, and white-water rafting.

Additional Tips:

- The weather in Val Verzasca can change rapidly, so be sure to check the forecast before heading out on a hike or other outdoor activity.

- Be prepared for steep terrain and challenging hikes.

- Dress appropriately for the weather and put on comfy shoes.

Embrace the Beauty of Val Verzasca

A visit to Val Verzasca is an invitation to immerse yourself in the valley's stunning scenery, rich natural beauty, and charming villages. Whether you're seeking a relaxing getaway in the Alps, an outdoor adventure, or simply a chance to experience a unique corner of Switzerland, Val Verzasca has something to offer everyone.

Jura Mountains

The Jura Mountains, a captivating natural wonder spanning eastern France and northwestern Switzerland, stand as a testament to the geological forces that have shaped this breathtaking region. These sub-alpine mountains, stretching for approximately 300 kilometers (186 miles), are renowned for their diverse landscapes, rich history, and ecological significance.

The Jura Mountains offer a haven for nature enthusiasts, providing a tapestry of diverse landscapes that captivate the senses. Hikers and mountaineers relish the challenge of trekking through verdant forests, navigating rugged terrain, and conquering towering peaks. Cyclists relish the exhilaration of winding through scenic valleys and conquering rolling hills, while those seeking water-based adventures can embark on kayaking or canoeing expeditions along the region's tranquil rivers and lakes.

Important Information to Keep in Mind When Visiting

Getting There:

The Jura Mountains are easily accessible by train from major cities in both France and Switzerland. International airports in Geneva, Zurich, and Basel provide connections to cities worldwide.

Accommodation:

A wide range of accommodation options is available throughout the Jura Mountains, from luxurious hotels and cozy bed and breakfasts to budget-friendly hostels and campsites.

Activities:

In addition to hiking, biking, and kayaking, the Jura Mountains offer a variety of activities, including rock climbing, spelunking, and cultural attractions.

Additional Tips:

- Learn a few basic French phrases, as French is the primary language spoken in the region.

- Check the weather conditions before planning your trip, as they can change rapidly in the mountains.

- Dress appropriately for the conditions, and be sure to wear comfortable shoes for walking and hiking.

Embrace the Enchantment of the Jura Mountains

A journey through the Jura Mountains is an invitation to immerse yourself in a world of natural wonders, cultural riches, and serene tranquility. Whether you're seeking invigorating outdoor adventures, captivating cultural experiences, or simply a peaceful escape amidst the mountains, the Jura Mountains offer a symphony of experiences that will leave you feeling refreshed, inspired, and deeply connected to the essence of this enchanting region.

CHAPTER SIX: OVERVIEW OF SWISS CUISINE

Swiss cuisine is a delightful fusion of traditional Alpine recipes, hearty mountain fare, and influences from neighboring countries like Germany, France, and Italy. The cuisine varies across regions, showcasing unique specialties and local ingredients.

Popular Swiss Dishes and Specialties

Rösti:

Rösti is a classic Swiss dish made from grated potatoes that are pan-fried until golden and crispy. It's often served as a side dish accompanying meats or topped with ingredients like cheese, bacon, or eggs for a heartier meal.

Fondue:

Switzerland is famous for its cheese fondue, a communal dish where a pot of melted cheese—typically a blend of Gruyère and Emmental—is served with cubes of bread for dipping. Fondue is a social meal enjoyed with friends or family.

Raclette:

Raclette is another beloved cheese dish. Traditionally, a wheel of Raclette cheese is heated, and the melted cheese is scraped onto plates, usually served with boiled potatoes, pickles, and onions.

Zürcher Geschnetzeltes:

Zürcher Geschnetzeltes is a Zurich specialty consisting of sliced veal in a creamy mushroom sauce, often accompanied by Rösti or pasta.

Älplermagronen:

Älplermagronen, also known as Swiss Alpine macaroni, is a comforting dish featuring macaroni, potatoes, cheese, onions, and often served with applesauce.

Swiss Chocolate:

Switzerland is renowned for its high-quality chocolate. Swiss chocolate, made from premium cocoa beans, is a treat not to be missed. Visitors can explore chocolate factories and indulge in various types of chocolates, pralines, and truffles.

Zopf:

Zopf is a traditional Swiss bread, braided and often consumed on Sundays or special occasions. It has a rich flavor and slightly sweet taste, making it a breakfast favorite.

Considerations

- **Regional Variations:** Swiss cuisine varies across regions. For example, French-influenced cuisine is prevalent in western Switzerland, while German influences are more pronounced in the central and northern regions.

- **Seasonal Specialties:** Depending on the season, Swiss cuisine embraces seasonal ingredients such as Alpine cheeses, fresh berries, and game meats, offering different specialties throughout the year.

- **Local Markets and Festivals:** Visiting local markets or attending food festivals provides opportunities to taste authentic Swiss dishes, sample local produce, and experience the diversity of Swiss gastronomy.

- **Wine and Dairy Products:** Switzerland is also known for its excellent wines, especially in the Valais and Lake Geneva regions. Additionally, the country produces a wide variety of cheeses, each with its distinct flavor profile.

Recommended Restaurants and Cafés

Zurich:

- **Kronenhalle:** A historic Zurich restaurant known for its classic Swiss cuisine and an impressive art collection adorning its walls.

- **Sprüngli:** Famous for its luxurious chocolates and delectable pastries, Sprüngli is a must-visit café in Zurich for sweet indulgences.

Geneva:

- **Les Armures:** This restaurant in Geneva's Old Town offers a cozy ambiance and serves traditional Swiss cuisine, including fondue and raclette.

- **Café du Soleil:** A charming café with a terrace offering a selection of Swiss and French dishes in a relaxed setting.

Lucerne:

- **Old Swiss House:** Known for its historic setting and exceptional Swiss specialties like veal Zurich-style and mouthwatering desserts.

- **Mill'Feuille:** A delightful café in Lucerne serving excellent coffee and homemade pastries.

Local Markets and Street Foods

Markets:

- **Zurich Farmers' Market (Zürcher Bauernmarkt):** Held on Bürkliplatz, this market offers fresh produce, regional cheeses, and local specialties.

- **Bern Farmer's Market (Bern Wochenmarkt):** Located on Bundesplatz, it showcases Swiss produce, artisanal goods, and a variety of regional delicacies.

Street Foods:

- **Bratwurst:** Swiss sausages like Bratwurst are a common street food. Try them from local stands or food trucks in cities and towns.

- **Raclette Sandwiches:** Some food stalls offer raclette cheese melted and served on bread or with potatoes, a delightful on-the-go treat.

- **Läckerli:** A traditional Swiss gingerbread, often found at local bakeries or street markets, perfect for a sweet snack.

Considerations

- **Seasonal Markets:** Check for seasonal markets or festivals offering regional specialties or themed culinary events, showcasing the diversity of Swiss cuisine.

- **Local Recommendations:** Engage with locals or tour guides for recommendations on hidden eateries, food markets, or street food hotspots that might not be listed in guidebooks.

- **Hygiene and Authenticity:** When trying street food, ensure cleanliness and opt for vendors preparing food on the spot using fresh ingredients for an authentic culinary experience.

- **Café Culture:** Embrace the café culture in Switzerland by indulging in coffee and pastries at local cafes, enjoying the relaxed atmosphere and observing the local way of life.

CHAPTER SEVEN: EXPERIENCES AND ACTIVITIES IN SWITZERLAND

Adventure Sports

Skiing and Snowboarding

Switzerland is a paradise for winter sports enthusiasts. World-class ski resorts like Zermatt, Verbier, and St. Moritz offer pristine slopes, powdery snow, and a range of skiing and snowboarding opportunities suitable for beginners to expert-level enthusiasts.

Hiking and Mountaineering

The Swiss Alps provide a plethora of hiking trails catering to all levels of hikers. From leisurely walks along scenic paths to challenging alpine treks, hikers can explore breathtaking landscapes, serene valleys, and iconic peaks like the Eiger, Mönch, and Jungfrau.

Cycling and Mountain Biking

Switzerland's well-maintained cycling routes and mountain biking trails offer thrilling experiences. The country boasts picturesque routes like the Rhine Route and the Alpine Panorama Route, catering to cyclists of varying abilities.

Paragliding and Skydiving

Adventurers can experience the thrill of paragliding or skydiving amidst Switzerland's stunning landscapes. Interlaken and Lauterbrunnen are popular spots for paragliding, offering aerial views of lakes, mountains, and valleys.

Cultural Experiences

Traditional Festivals and Events

- **Fasnacht (Carnival):** Celebrated across different regions, Fasnacht is a lively pre-Lenten carnival featuring colorful parades, masked revelers, and traditional music and dances. Basel's Fasnacht is particularly renowned.

- **Zurich Street Parade:** This electronic dance music festival in Zurich draws thousands of participants and spectators to dance through the city streets.

- **Swiss National Day:** Celebrated on August 1st, Swiss National Day offers a chance to witness traditional ceremonies, fireworks, and cultural events throughout the country.

Museums and Cultural Sites

- **Château de Chillon:** Besides being an iconic landmark, this castle hosts cultural events, exhibitions, and guided tours, providing insights into Swiss history and heritage.

- **Rütli Meadow:** Known as the birthplace of Switzerland, Rütli Meadow on Lake Lucerne is where the Swiss Confederation was formed in 1291. Visitors can experience Swiss history in this historic setting.

- **Cultural Performances:** Attend classical music concerts, opera performances, or folk music events, showcasing Switzerland's rich musical heritage.

Considerations

- **Seasonal Variations:** Plan activities based on the season to enjoy specific sports or cultural events, as some activities might be weather-dependent.

- **Local Guides and Tours:** Engage with local guides or join tours to gain deeper insights into cultural events, historical sites, and to access off-the-beaten-path experiences.

- **Equipment and Safety:** For adventure sports, ensure proper equipment, and consider taking lessons or guided tours, especially for activities like skiing, paragliding, or mountain biking.

Shopping Guide

Swiss Watches:

Renowned for precision and craftsmanship, Swiss watches are a popular souvenir. Brands like Rolex, Omega, and

Swatch offer a range of options from luxury to more affordable timepieces.

Swiss Chocolates:

Swiss chocolates are an iconic souvenir. Opt for assortments from renowned chocolatiers like Lindt, Toblerone, or visit local chocolatiers for handmade chocolates with unique flavors.

Swiss Cheese:

Varieties like Gruyère, Emmental, and Appenzeller make for flavorful and authentic Swiss gifts. Buy from local markets or cheese shops for a taste of traditional Swiss cheese.

Swiss Army Knives:

Victorinox and Wenger produce the famous Swiss Army Knives. These versatile tools make practical and iconic souvenirs, available in various sizes and designs.

Swiss Handicrafts:

Explore Swiss handicrafts such as intricate wood carvings, hand-painted ceramics, traditional textiles like embroidered linens, and delicate lacework, available at local artisan shops.

Nightlife and Entertainment in Swiss Cities

Zurich:

Zurich offers a vibrant nightlife scene with a range of bars, clubs, and lounges. Langstrasse is known for its diverse nightlife, while areas like Niederdorf provide cozy bars and live music venues.

Geneva:

Geneva boasts a refined nightlife with cocktail bars, jazz clubs, and waterfront lounges. Rue de l'École-de-Médecine and Carouge are popular areas for bars and entertainment.

Basel:

Basel's nightlife includes a mix of cultural venues, bars, and clubs. The Kleinbasel area along the Rhine offers hip bars, while Marktplatz has traditional Swiss taverns.

Lausanne:

Lausanne offers a lively nightlife scene with bars overlooking Lake Geneva, jazz clubs, and nightclubs. Flon and Ouchy are popular areas for entertainment.

Considerations

- **Local Markets and Boutiques:** Explore local markets and boutique stores for authentic and unique souvenirs crafted by local artisans.

- **Safety and Enjoyment:** While enjoying nightlife, be mindful of personal safety and adhere to local norms and regulations for a pleasant experience.

- **Event Calendars:** Check event calendars or local listings for concerts, cultural events, and festivals happening during your visit to experience Swiss entertainment and cultural richness.

- **Public Transportation:** Swiss cities often have reliable public transportation, making it convenient to navigate between nightlife spots.

CHAPTER EIGHT: PRACTICAL INFORMATION
Safety and Security Tips

- **Low Crime Rate:** Switzerland is generally safe, with a low crime rate. However, exercise caution in crowded tourist areas to prevent pickpocketing or petty theft.

- **Protect Valuables:** Keep your belongings secure and avoid leaving personal items unattended, especially in crowded places, public transport, and tourist spots.

- **Emergency Numbers:** The general emergency number in Switzerland is 112 for police, ambulance, and fire services. Dialing 117 specifically connects to the police.

- **Mountain Safety:** If engaging in outdoor activities in the mountains, check weather forecasts, adhere to trail markings, and inform someone about your itinerary. Follow safety guidelines for hiking, skiing, and mountain sports.

- **COVID-19 Safety Measures:** Stay updated on COVID-19 guidelines and regulations, including mask mandates, social distancing rules, and vaccination requirements. Follow local health authorities' recommendations.

Health Precautions

- **Travel Insurance:** Obtain comprehensive travel insurance that includes repatriation and coverage for medical emergencies.

- **Healthcare System:** Switzerland has excellent healthcare facilities, but medical expenses can be high. Ensure you have adequate insurance coverage.

- **Routine Vaccinations:** Ensure routine vaccinations are up-to-date. Depending on the season and regions visited, additional vaccinations might be recommended. Consult your physician prior to departure.

- **Water Quality:** Tap water is safe to drink throughout Switzerland. To remain hydrated, have a reusable water bottle with you.

Emergency Contacts

- **Emergency Services:** Dial 112 for general emergencies or 117 for police assistance.

- **Medical Emergencies:** In case of medical emergencies, dial 144 for an ambulance.

- **Fire Department:** Dial 118 to report fires or request firefighting services.

- **Helpline for Tourists:** For non-emergency assistance and information for tourists, call the Swiss Tourist Helpline at +41 43 210 5512.

- **Embassy Contacts:** Know the contact details and location of your country's embassy or consulate in Switzerland for assistance in case of emergencies or lost documents.

Considerations

- **Local Customs and Laws:** Familiarize yourself with local customs and laws to respect cultural norms and avoid unintentional breaches.

- **Language:** While English is widely spoken, especially in tourist areas, learning basic phrases in German, French, or Italian can be helpful, depending on the region.

- **Travel Alerts:** Stay updated on travel advisories and alerts from your country's embassy or consulate before and during your trip.

Language Basics

Useful Phrases

Swiss German (Zurich/Basel dialects)

- **Hello:** Grüezi (Grew-tsi)

- **Goodbye:** Adieu (Ah-dee-oo)

- **Please:** Bitte (Bitt-uh)

- **Thank you:** Merci vilmal (Mehr-see feel-mahl)

- **Yes:** Ja (Yah)

- **No:** Nei (Nay)

- **Excuse me:** Entschuldigung (Ent-shool-dih-gung)

- **Do you speak English?:** Spreched Sie Engländer? (Spray-ked zee Eng-lan-der?)

- **How much does it cost?:** Wie viel koscht das? (Vee feel kohsht dahs?)

French

- **Hello:** Bonjour (Bon-zhoor)

- **Goodbye:** Au revoir (O re-vwar)

- **Please:** S'il vous plaît (Seel voo pleh)

- **Thank you:** Merci (Mehr-see)

- **Yes:** Oui (Wee)

- **No:** Non (Noh)

- **Excuse me:** Excusez-moi (Ex-kew-zay mwa)

- **Do you speak English?:** Parlez-vous anglais? (Par-lay voo on-glay?)

- **How much does it cost?:** Combien ça coûte? (Kohm-byen sah koot?)

Italian

- **Hello:** Ciao (Chow)

- **Goodbye:** Arrivederci (Ah-ree-veh-dehr-chee)

- **Please:** Per favore (Pair fah-voh-ray)

- **Thank you:** Grazie (Graht-see-eh)

- **Yes:** Sì (See)

- **No:** No (No)

- **Excuse me:** Mi scusi (Mee skoo-zee)

- **Do you speak English?:** Parla inglese? (Par-la een-gleh-zeh?)

- **How much does it cost?:** Quanto costa? (Kwan-toh koh-stah?)

Currency and Money Matters

- **Currency:** Switzerland's currency is Swiss Franc (CHF). Symbol: CHF or Fr. Coins come in denominations of 5, 10, 20, and 50 centimes, and 1, 2, and 5 Francs. Banknotes are in denominations of 10, 20, 50, 100, 200, and 1,000 Francs.

- **Exchange Rates:** Check current exchange rates before exchanging money or making purchases to understand the value of the Swiss Franc in your home currency.

- **Credit Cards and ATMs:** Credit cards are widely accepted, but it's advisable to carry some cash, especially in smaller towns or for small purchases. ATMs (called "Bancomat" in Switzerland) are widely available.

- **Tipping:** Tipping is not mandatory but appreciated for good service. Service charges are often included in restaurant bills, but rounding up the amount is customary.

- **Tax Refunds:** Non-resident travelers can apply for a VAT refund on eligible purchases made in Switzerland. Look for the Tax-Free Shopping logo and request a tax refund form when making purchases.

CHAPTER NINE: INSIDER TIPS AND RECOMMENDATIONS

Local Insights and Recommendations

Explore Local Cuisine:

- **Try Regional Specialties:** Each Swiss region boasts its own culinary specialties. Don't miss the chance to taste raclette in the Valais, fondue in Fribourg, or Zürcher Geschnetzeltes in Zurich for an authentic experience.

- **Visit Local Markets:** Explore local markets to sample artisanal cheeses, fresh produce, and handmade crafts while interacting with locals. Farmer's markets offer a glimpse into Swiss daily life.

Off-the-Beaten-Path Locations:

- **Discover Smaller Towns:** While cities like Zurich and Geneva are captivating, consider exploring smaller towns like Gruyères, Murten, or Lauterbrunnen for a more intimate Swiss experience and fewer crowds.

- **Hidden Gems:** Delve into hidden valleys, lesser-known hiking trails, or scenic spots like Lake Cauma in Graubünden or the Aare Gorge near Meiringen for serene natural beauty.

Cultural Immersion:

- **Attend Local Festivals:** Check the local calendar for festivals and events. Whether it's a traditional Alpabzug (cattle descent) or a wine festival, these events provide insight into Swiss culture and traditions.

- **Engage with Locals:** Strike up conversations with locals at cafés, markets, or cultural events. Swiss people are often friendly and willing to share insights about their country.

Outdoor Adventures:

- **Sunrise or Sunset Views:** Head to mountain peaks like Mount Pilatus, Schilthorn, or Rigi for breathtaking sunrise or sunset views amidst the Alps.

- **Seasonal Activities:** Embrace seasonal activities like skiing in winter, hiking or paragliding in summer, or exploring colorful autumn foliage in the Swiss countryside.

Transportation Tips:

- **Swiss Travel Pass:** Consider purchasing a Swiss Travel Pass for unlimited travel on trains, buses, and boats, offering convenience and flexibility for exploring various regions.

- **Scenic Train Routes:** Experience picturesque train journeys like the Glacier Express, Bernina Express, or

Golden Pass Line, offering stunning vistas of Swiss landscapes.

Dos and Don'ts for Travelers in Switzerland

Dos for Travelers in Switzerland

- **Greet with Courtesy:** Use polite greetings such as "Grüezi" in German-speaking regions, "Bonjour" in French-speaking areas, or "Buongiorno" in Italian-speaking areas. Politeness is highly valued in Swiss culture.

- **Punctuality:** Swiss people highly appreciate punctuality. Whether it's meeting friends, attending tours, or catching public transport, arriving on time is essential.

- **Respect Personal Space:** Swiss people value personal space and privacy. Maintain an appropriate distance while interacting and respect boundaries.

- **Follow Recycling and Cleanliness:** Switzerland is known for its cleanliness and commitment to recycling. Follow recycling guidelines and keep public spaces clean.

- **Treat Nature Respectfully:** Switzerland is blessed with stunning landscapes. When hiking or exploring nature, follow designated trails, avoid littering, and respect wildlife.

- **Dress Appropriately:** Dress modestly and appropriately for various situations, especially when visiting religious sites or dining at upscale restaurants.

Don'ts for Travelers in Switzerland:

- **Avoid Being Loud:** Swiss people generally appreciate quiet and tend to speak softly in public places. Avoid loud conversations, especially on public transport or in restaurants.

- **Don't Be Late:** Punctuality is highly valued in Swiss culture. Avoid being late for appointments or scheduled meetings.

- **Don't Forget to Say "Thank You":** Express gratitude by saying "thank you" ("Merci" in French, "Danke" in German, or "Grazie" in Italian) in various situations.

- **Don't Discuss Politics or Religion Casually:** Avoid initiating discussions about politics or religion, especially with strangers, as these topics can be sensitive.

- **Don't Disregard Quiet Hours:** Many Swiss cities and towns have designated quiet hours, usually in the evenings or on Sundays. Respect these times and avoid making excessive noise.

- **Don't Forget to Tip Appropriately:** While tipping is not mandatory, it's appreciated for good service. Rounding up the bill or leaving a small tip is customary.

Swiss Etiquette and Cultural Norms

- **Swiss Directness:** Swiss people are known for their direct communication style. They value honesty and straightforwardness in conversations.

- **Respect for Rules:** Swiss society operates on a foundation of respect for rules and regulations. Following rules is considered a sign of respect for others.

- **Conservative Behavior:** Swiss culture tends to be conservative. While it's a modern and liberal society, exhibiting reserved behavior is common, especially in public settings.

- **Language Preferences:** Depending on the region, people speak German, French, Italian, or Romansh. While many Swiss speak English, making an effort to use basic phrases in their local language is appreciated.

conclusion

Congratulations, fellow traveler! You've reached the end of this delightful guide to Switzerland, the land of cheese, chocolates, and picture-perfect vistas! I hope you've enjoyed this rollercoaster ride through the Swiss Alps and the charming towns that make this country a traveler's dream.

From the dizzying heights of Jungfraujoch to the tranquil beauty of Lake Geneva, I've tried my best to serve up a Swiss buffet of information – from hiking trails to fondue secrets – to make your adventure as smooth as Swiss chocolate.

As you bid adieu to this guide, take with you memories of cowbell serenades, breathtaking mountain peaks, and the lingering taste of creamy raclette. Remember, it's not just about ticking off tourist spots; it's about savoring every moment – even the ones where you mispronounce "Grüezi" or get lost in a chocolate shop maze (trust me, it happens).

Before you pack your bags and head off on your Swiss escapade, here's a parting gift – a reminder to embrace the Swiss spirit: be punctual like Swiss trains, take in nature's splendor like a Swiss cow admiring the Alps, and always keep a stash of Swiss chocolate for emergencies (because, well, chocolate is the answer to everything).

I want to extend my heartfelt thanks for choosing this guide to accompany you on your Swiss adventure. May your travels be filled with laughter, discovery, and delightful encounters – and may you return home with stories that make your friends green with envy (or maybe just green with jealousy).

Remember, in the words of the wise Swiss mountain goats (probably), "Life's a mountain, climb it with a smile!"

Auf Wiedersehen and happy travels!

Printed in Great Britain
by Amazon

39509921R00059